My Secret Life

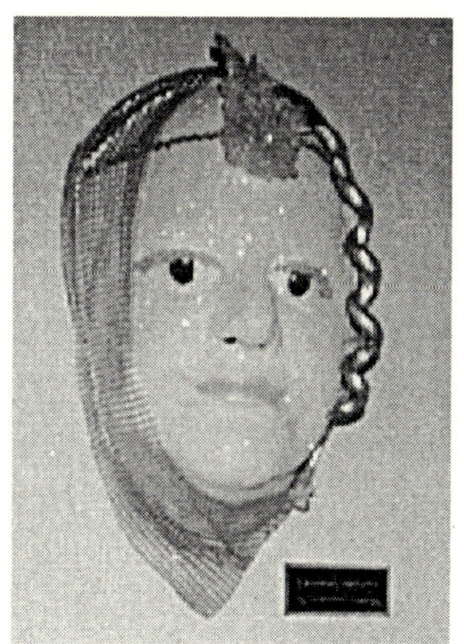

as a "Priestess"

Mask Created by:
LIZ LEARMONT
*Artist * Mask Maker*

<u>**Dedication**</u>

To *Marcelle*, the mother of my body and to *Saint Barbara*, the mother of my soul, my sincere thanks to you both for the love and support you've given me throughout my life.

To *Albert*, father of my body I say "thank you" for that twinkle in your eye and your seed that begot my being. "Thank you" for watching over me in death as you did in life: you will always have my undying love and respect.

To *John Charles,* my soul mate, and "spiritual godfather, as time goes on my gratitude to you grows and grows, more each day. You are the one who opened the gateway to the other side for me. You are the one who guides my spirit to ensure that I remain safe and attached to this plane of existence.

You have proven Shakespeare right when he said that there are more things on earth, than in heaven. More that I could have ever dreamed of.

Presented by the *Turbane Company*

ISBN#   978-0-6151-5015-4

My Secret Life

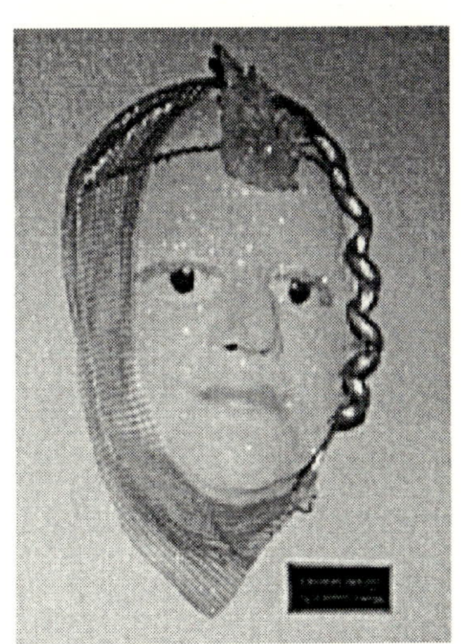

as a " Priestess "

By

Ronnie Gale Turbane

TABLE OF CONTENTS

Introduction ....: pg. 10
My Search Begins.... pg. 13
Still Searching......... pg. 23
Enter JOHN......... pg. 35
Saint Barbara......... pg. 57
Orientation........... pg. 75
Back to Reality....... pg. 87
Ronnie, Daughter of *Saint Barbara*,
Priestess of Chango...... pg. 99
Invitation to "MASS.... pg. 125
If He can, I can to........ pg. 145
Help, I need HELP..... pg. 159
My gift to YOU......... pg. 185

INTRODUCTION

Dear Reader,

Were you born with the same mindset as I? If, you were, throughout your life you have asked yourself the following questions.

Who am I?

Where did I come from?

Why am I here?

Where am I going?

What will become of me?

Is this "all" there really is?

Am I alone?

Though it may seem unbelievable to you, I have found a path in life that gives me peace on earth. It enables me to have the strength to live each day without fear. It allows me to help my fellow man/woman.

I now live my life knowing that this is simply a "learning experience" meant to bring us closer to **GOD**.

We are all merely threads woven into the "*fabric of life*".

Our journey begins when we are born into an *essence* called humanity. Quickly, our emotions, our feelings, our senses take root, and then we begin to grow. As we age, everything we've experienced is absorbed into our bodies and imprinted onto our souls. Too soon, we then return to where we first began. It is there that we share the infinite wisdom and knowledge of the *life lessons* we've learned with our **GOD**.

We then return to Earths' plane of existence over and over again. Our *eternal soul* remains in a state of perpetuity until our own individual personal quest is complete.

This I have learned.

This I know is true.

I walk the path of GOD.

I was told that YOU may now follow me on my journey.

<u>MY SEARCH BEGINS</u>

When I was a young woman it seemed that my "life" was filled with many unanswered questions. I wondered why I was here living on this planet we call earth. In my early years, I truly thought that I needed material things to be happy in my everyday life.

But now, in this moment of time, I say to you that there is a true *"fabric of life"*. One of which I will help you to embrace and to learn about in this book.

This is my gift to YOU. For I have found my peace as I walk the path to *enlightenment*.

In my younger years I was a sci-fi groupie. I watched movies and television episodes of every show that related to the paranormal. I read books about the *"other side"*. I followed the teachings of every psychic and mystic I heard of. For many years my friends and I scheduled visits to clairvoyants that we thought could and would give us the answers to our questions. We "needed" to know what was going to happen to us in our lives. We "wanted" to know at that moment in time if we would each find love and happiness; sooner rather than later.

When a woman visits a psychic she asks if love and marriage are destined for her in life. When a man visits a mystic he wants to know if money and power are in his future.

I have many fond memories of those youthful days.

Once I was told by a psychic to follow the path of the psychics, because I too was really *"one of them"*. When I was in my early twenties, two girlfriends and I visited a well known reader who lived in the same town where we worked. She led us one by one into a small room which was situated off her dining area. When I entered the room I saw that she had an altar set up. The room was full of life size *Saints*. I sat down and immediately I began to sweat. I became physically ill. She gave me a glass of water to help calm me down. Once I calmed down, she began my reading. She told me that I was a very spiritual being and that someday I would learn about life's true meaning. At that time she said I would follow a new path. She was very specific in the things that she said to me next.

Please remember, here I was, a woman in my early twenties. I was looking for love. I was hoping to get married. I wanted everything that I'm very sure every young woman at that time in her early twenties thought she needed to have in order to be happy. I wanted validation in the eyes of society and of course in the eyes of my *girlfriends*.

I was surprised that what I was hearing from this clairvoyant did not sound like something she would recite from a standard script written for *"single young females"*. She told me that I would **NOT** find true love for a very long time. She said that I would have to wait for my <u>social security</u> days to have a man walk beside me. Together, he and I would walk life's path with love and happiness surrounding us.

But, she said I would have to wait. For then and only then, in a future that seemed distant and so far away, would I ever be able to meet my significant other. This would be the person that I had been waiting for all my life.

It sounded like my life partner WAS a lifetime away.

She said that I would meet him while I was visiting at a friend's house. My friend would have light eyes. While I would be at my friend's house, my future *significant other* would also be stopping by to pay a visit. He will have had just ended a relationship. He will be immediately attracted to me. He will have sandy brown hair and light brown eyes. After my visit is over and I leave, he will ask my friend for my phone number.

He will contact me soon after.

Well, you can just imagine how I felt. I was pleased. I was shocked. I was disappointed and I was getting very impatient. I had an array of emotions going through my head, all at the same time. I was really glad that she gave me answers to my questions. Though why did I have to wait for my *"social security days"* before I could find "true love".

Everyone in my circle of girlfriends was either engaged or they had plans to get married, at that moment in time, in the next year or two. None of them had to wait for years and years to find their life partner. I was the only one left of my peer group who was NOT in a serious relationship, was NOT dating, and was NOT engaged. I was NOT a happy camper.

Why did I have to wait?

By the time my reading was over I was totally depressed.

Well, I guess you're asking by now, did I ever did meet the sandy haired man? I tell you now, the answer is NO. It is Thursday, June 7th 2007, 10:11 A.M., *EST* and I'm still waiting.

I will tell you a secret though. For the next few years whenever I received an invitation to go to a friend's house, I asked myself what color their eyes were. If my friend had light eyes, quick like a bunny I was there paying a visit.

If YOU happen to see my SHSO (sandy hair significant other), please tell him to hurry up and get to me soon.

Is he stuck in traffic?

What could be taking him so long to find me?

Oh well, I have not yet reached my social security status. So, I will wait a bit longer for him. I don't ever want to stop hoping and dreaming. I wonder if by the time I meet him his hair will be grey or still sandy brown. I say that because by that time, I'm sure I'll be losing most of mine.

Let me now continue.

During the following years, I carried on with my quest to attain insight on what the true meaning of life was. I knew that "*knowledge is power*", so I connected with everyone I heard about that I thought might awaken something inside me and give me peace of mind.

As time passed on my resolve did remain firm. But, I must say that my hope for answers about the existence of life had dimmed. I would drive to Atlantic City, N.J. and see fortune tellers on the boardwalk. I traveled to Sedona, AZ. (*the New Age Center of the World*) to have readings with the telepathic.

My sister Marilyn gave me a special gift. She arranged a session for me with *Artist-Mask maker, Liz Learmont* to have a *"life mask"* created.

This experience touched the essence of my body and mind. I told Liz, *"it felt like I was having a* ***facial for the soul"***.

STILL SEARCHING

As I moved on in life, I realized how lucky I was. I lived at home with my mother, my father, my sister and my grandfather. We were a close knit family group who loved each other very much. We always took very good care of each other. I was loved and protected.

At work I was happy, my good luck continued and my accomplishments were many. I moved up the ladder of success easily. I had a great reputation and a wonderful business career. I had a diverse group of friends that I enjoyed being with. I had plenty of money available to me and I traveled often. I believed that the office location I worked in actually brought me much good luck. My life seemed to be reflecting off its name, *"**Lake Success**"*.

Finding men to date was easy. I fell in love often. In a fleeting moment I did think I had found "true love". But, as quickly as it began, it ended, he left and once again I was alone. A long-lasting, loving relationship and marriage continued to elude me.

In my most private moments, I would say to myself, "Ronnie, don't worry, you'll find your true love someday. You just might have to wait until for your *social security days*".

Then, even I would laugh aloud. I did continue to have one ongoing mystic connection. I used the *Ouija board* often, in hopes of contacting someone on the "other side". No one here seemed to be able to help me. So, I was hoping someone out there could and would offer help.

The *Ouija board* is defined as a trademark for a board with letters and a pointer by which answers to questions are spelled out, supposedly by *spiritual forces.*

I had read that the *Ouija board* was quite popular during wartime when women would buy them and try to contact their loved ones who were thought to be lost overseas.

Using the *Ouija board* can easily and quickly become addictive. I was actually taking my *Ouija board* to bed with me each night. After much practice, I had learned how to work the *Ouija board* by myself. My heart, not my head, made me believe that I was in constant contact with the forces of "*good, not evil*".

What I did learn after a time is that the *Ouija board* is NOT a toy or a game. It is actually a very strong <u>means</u> by which you can connect to and communicate with the energies on the "other side". The *Ouija board* quickly becomes a doorway to another dimension.

This is a place inhabited by both negative and positive *energies* and *essences*.

People **MUST** be aware of this and prepare themselves with protection **BEFORE** they dabble in something that they truly do not understand.

If you spend too much time using the *Ouija board* you may have negative results on your emotional and physical self. You see, many people are more "*spiritually open*" than they know. When your mind, spirit and soul are exposed to outside forces, you **MUST** be ready to protect yourself and not allow something to attach itself to your body's essence. In certain circles when this happens it is referred to as being "*possessed*".

I remember one time I took my *Ouija board* to a friend's house. We expected to have a fun night and make memories with *Ouija board* stories that we would tell others about. After dinner, we took the *Ouija board* to her parents' bedroom and placed it in the center of the bed. We brought snacks onto the bed with us and began asking the *Ouija board* question after question. The pointer began moving quickly. It not only answered our questions, it started **ASKING** us questions. The questions started to get personal and very embarrassing. We both got really very nervous.

Then, (I can't believe I'm telling you this. To this day, I still can't believe it really happened), the bed started **SHAKING**.

Honestly, it did!

We got so scared. We both jumped off the bed and ran out of the bedroom. After a while I went back into the room to get the *Ouija board*. I put the *Ouija board* in a brown paper bag and then I walked it out to my car. I was still kind of shaky and frightened so I locked the *Ouija board* in car trunk.

I know this may sound really dumb, but this incident actually made me more curious about spiritual beings. Now I knew that they really exist. So, that night I decided to continue with my search for answers to my "unanswered" questions about life.

By now, I was not only intrigued by, but obsessed with, the paranormal.

I found out about a course in paranormal experiences being given at a local college. I signed up for the course. The time seemed right for the paranormal.

It was going main stream and I was going to go along for the ride.

My sister Marilyn was kind enough to join me on my weekly drive to the college course. Though, the paranormal was not Marilyn's cup of tea, she did sign up for a cooking class on the same night so I would not have to travel to the college alone.

I was anxious and excited to think that I was finally going to learn about the *secrets of the universe.*

Each week the teacher spoke on a different subject matter; ghosts, visitations, healings, out-of-body experiences, etc. After a while I became disenchanted with her delivery on so many different topics. I thought I knew more about these areas of interest than even she did.

A few weeks later, Marilyn told me that a local high school was having a night course on *bio-rhythm*. This was something new for me to ponder. So, I signed up and took the course. Soon, I immersed myself in all the material I could find about bio-rhythm. I became quite educated on the topic. The logic and definitive results it provided amazed me.

I bought a bio-rhythm machine. I became an expert on creating charts on a person's daily "pre-destined" results for a certain day in time. My accuracy was amazing. One day I decided to make a business proposal about the use of bio-rhythms to the District Manager of the Sales department. I told him about all the research I had done. I explained to him that in Japan, many companies were creating bio-rhythm charts daily for their employees. They would then align the employee's daily bio-rhythm results to their business needs.

The idea interested him. I generated a few charts on his salesman for the following few days by using their birth dates. The manager was truly fascinated with the data I provided to him for review.

A few days later he told me that he had thought about my theories fully and decided he could NOT use the concept.

He felt that every member of his sales staff MUST have a

positive attitude each and every day. It is crucial for them to give of themselves, 100%, 24/7, thinking that success is theirs to achieve on a daily basis. He could not and would not allow anything to present a negative "slant" on their daily performance. Not even for one pre-destined negative bio-rhythm day.

He of course meant that if a salesman was told that his/her bio-rhythms were not good on a certain day; he/she would not apply themselves to work fully on that day.

I guess you realize by now that I have an open mind when it comes to finding new avenues to explore.

I think I have a hunger to learn about things that will allow me to discover more about the "workings" of life on earth.

ENTER JOHN

During the next few years, the days quickly became weeks, the weeks swiftly became months and then the months abruptly changed into years. I was still working at Lake Success. I thought my life was as good as it would ever get. I still had many "unanswered" questions. But, I thought that when GOD wanted me to know more about **LIFE**, he/she would tell me themselves.

One day, I was told that a new employee named John was arriving to join the Loss Prevention Department staff. The department's work area was set up directly outside of my work area. I planned on welcoming this new arrival to "my" office. As the Office Manager, it was the norm for me to introduce myself as part of a new hire's orientation.

When I first saw John I was immediately impressed with his good looks, professional appearance and demeanor. He had a charismatic personality. I saw that he treated every member of the staff with dignity and respect from day one. This was not always the case because often technical employees would think that the clerical staff was "beneath" them and that they were only employed to do the techs' personal bidding.

John was 24 years of age when I first met him. He was a single, young, Cuban-American. He was highly educated. He had excellent credentials in the field of chemical engineering and he was obviously worldly beyond his years. I learned that his family had fled Cuba for America in the days when Castro first took power. They were members of the country's elite class.

His mother's people were part of the aristocrats of the land and his father's side had lineage back to a very famous, world renowned artist.

John was a gentleman to every female in the office and he quickly developed a "female" following. He seemed to be able to sense what everyone not just wanted, but what people actually needed.

Almost immediately he tried to develop a friendship with me. I was a bit surprised. I knew every employee in the office by name and I was on good terms with ALL of them. But, I believed in keeping my personal life separate and apart from my work life.

Except for Laura, an older female retiree who returned to work as a part-time employee, I did not socialize with anyone in the office. I also had never developed personal friendships with younger men.

John made it a point to stop by my office each day when he arrived at work. He would also stop by and say good night to me on his way out of the office each and every evening.

Soon he was having his coffee breaks at my desk daily. We chatted about a million different things. I truly began to look forward to his visits day after day.

As I got to know John, I started to like him more and more. He was younger than me but we seem to have so very many things in common. Our beliefs about life were the same. We were alike. Our friendship grew and grew. Our conversations covered every area of work life, spiritual life and life on the *"other side"*.

I soon realized that I had found someone who finally seemed to understand my need to have answers to all my questions about the meaning of life. John had a "grasp" of this knowledge that was far beyond his years.

Often, he would really get on my nerves. John seemed to think that <u>my</u> title, *Office Manager*, belonged to him. He frequently gave the clerical staff working in the Loss Prevention Department extra time for lunch without asking for my approval. He would advise me when "*he*" thought they needed overtime to complete their daily workloads.

One day I received a phone call from the local bank that my company did business with in "*Lake Success*". The bank representative said that they were calling on John's behalf. He had given my name, w/my title, as a reference so that he could open a new checking account for himself without delay.

When he returned to the office I quickly reprimanded him. I sat him down in my office and said, *"John, YOU are very COCKY"*. He turned, looked me straight in the eye and said, *"Turbane, we are going to be friends forever"*.

<u>That dear reader was almost 25 years ago.</u>

A few days later something happened at work that made me realize that John truly did have some type of spiritual connection to me. He actually knew how I felt about things.

We were both talking to a group of male Loss Prevention employees. They were telling stories and jokes and everyone was laughing. I knew these employees for years and they often included me in their personal conversations. The banter started to get risqué and I started to feel embarrassed.

Though I was the office manager, and I was the one who gave employees talks on sexual harassment and hostile work environment at the workplace, I stood standing there in silence. I did not reply and I did not laugh at the exchange.

I felt invisible.

I felt out of place.

Deep inside my head, I was really feeling very uncomfortable. At the exact moment that my humiliation kicked in I heard John say, *"Guys, we have a lady here. I think we need to stop now"*. Then he looked at me and he smiled. The conversation continued but the subject matter was immediately redirected to work issues.

No one noticed my reaction to the inappropriate talk.

No one seemed to care that I was even there.

No one that is, except for John.

At that exact moment I knew that what John had said to me awhile ago was going to be true. He and I *"were going to be friends forever"*.

Occasionally, Laura would join us for coffee breaks in my office. The three of us would talk about the many wonders that the world had to offer humanity. We even planned on taking a trip together and going to Rio De Janerio at festival time.

We shared many stories and told each other about private moments from our past. I told them of my encounter using the *Ouija board* and about my many visits to mystics.

John told us that he was open to all beliefs and that he also had used the *Ouija board*. He said that the Cuban culture follows a very spiritual path. This conversation interested my greatly. I asked John for more information. I wanted to know everything that he knew.

He invited Laura and me to visit him at his home over the weekend. We planned to go out for brunch and then return to his house for conversation on the paranormal and maybe, just maybe he would do a reading for us.

WHAT!

Did I hear him right?

Did John say he was psychic?

Did he say he could and would do readings for us? Wow!

Is he the answer to all my prayers?

Did he have the answers to my unanswered questions?

Did GOD send John to *Lake Success* just to meet me?

Laura and I waited anxiously for the weekend to arrive. We drove to see John on a Saturday. He was living in a six family house that he owned. He was one smart kid. He was street wise as well as money wise. This was not the first real estate property that he had owned.

I was very impressed.

Trump Towers, watch out!

Soon, there might be a John Towers.

When I was inside John's apartment, I noticed that he had many statues of Saints throughout the house. I was always intrigued by the Saints. I personally owned a beautiful statue of *Saint Anthony*. It was given to me by a nun who

Was part of a cloister order of nuns in Washington, D.C.

John brought out his *Ouija board* and we began a session. He then did as promised, he started a reading. We noticed that he went into the kitchen and returned with a water glass filled to the top with tap water. He placed it next to the *Ouija board*. I simply thought he expected to be thirsty and wanted to be ready with a drink of water by his hand.

As we continued, John seemed to control the movement and conversation of the session. Often he would look at the water and pick it up and look at it again. He did NOT drink from it though. Very curious, I thought, what was he doing?

When I asked, he said he felt comfortable enough to tell us about what he believes in and what religion he practiced.

He said he was getting his answers from the essence of the water. Yes, he said he was connecting with the energy being absorbed by the water. Water, the most powerful of all God's blessings, was what John used as a doorway to the other side. Who knew? I drank it. I bathed in it. I washed my car with it. Who knew?

John said he was a Spiritualist. He said that he was a son of *Saint Barbara* and a priest of *Chango*. I didn't have a clue of what he was talking about. I asked that he explain and he told us that in Cuba people were NOT allowed to practice religion freely. They had NO opportunity to go any house of GOD that they chose to.

Therefore, the people of Cuba follow a religion that was brought into Cuba from Africa. The religion is called Spiritualism. Its' followers believe in Catholic saints as deities and acknowledge them by calling them different names.

Cuba's most popular Saint followed is *Saint Barbara*.

I'm sure that at this moment you must be as intrigued as I was as to who *Saint Barbara* was and what she stood for. I had never heard about her. I had never known a Cuban American before. I was fascinated by all of this knowledge and I begged John to tell us more.

He began by telling us that he was baptized into the faith as a young child. This religion was filled with mysteries and power. It is, like all things in life, able to be used for both good and evil.

John was a Spiritualist. He made a point of telling us that he practiced only for good. He used candles, incense, cigars, coconuts, bells and water for offerings and secret rituals for each saint.

The saints are deities known as *The Seven African Powers.*

I learned that John had seen things in his life that I had only dreamed of.

John was able to speak to the Saints.

John could "*see*" the spirits of dead people.

John could see peoples' auras.

John often had visions of future events.

John knew ways of "*controlling*" future events.

John said that there was a way to end a person's life by using an old ritual from the religion. It would involve a graveyard, a chicken, a coconut and a ritual.

"Don't stop now John".

"More, more, tell me more John".

He continued to tell us that the only problem with taking someone's life by using a ritual is, that within seven days you forfeit your own life. He explained that there is a balance to all things in life. Ying and Yang, Good vs. Evil, you Reap what you Sow.

YOU get the picture.

I wanted to learn everything I could about *Saint Barbara*. I wanted to know everything I could about John's life. Could I too learn the secrets of life that John knew about?

I had oh so many questions going through my mind.

I asked John:

How is this possible?

Who are the chosen ones?

How does GOD choose them?

How can I meet *Saint Barbara*?

He looked directly at me and smiled. He said that it was *Saint Barbara* guided him to me. She had given him permission to approach me and show me their "*PATH*".

He said that all people are welcome to believe in *Saint Barbara*. He said that most will surely become her followers. He said that only a few chosen people are born "Spiritualists". These are the ones given a special gift from GOD. It is a gift that allows a person to walk the path of "*enlightenment*".

Well, need I say that my *life plan* was now kaput?

I thought that I was settled in a life style that suited me. I had made plans throughout the years to ensure that I would be comfortable and content. I accepted each and every day as is was.

But now, a quote comes to my mind that truly applies;

"If you want to make GOD laugh, make plans".

You now need to be more informed and educated about *Saint Barbara* before I can continue.

I will show you her *legend*, her *prayer* and her *novena*.

I will then explain the conviction of my belief in plain English. I will communicate by using my best method of communication; my own words.

I'm confident you will understand.

I'm confident you will believe.

SAINT BARBARA

Prayer:

O God, who among the other miracles of Your power have given even to the weaker sex the victory of martyrdom, grant we beseech You, that we, who are celebrating the heavenly birthday of Blessed Barbara, Your Virgin and Martyr, may, by her example, draw, nearer to you.

Amen.

<u>*Novena to Saint Barbara*</u>

Oh holy **Saint Barbara**

please hear this my prayer;

*for the truth I do speak
and my soul I do bare.*

The power of **CHANGO**
makes you mighty and strong;

*my petition to you is
from a heart that is torn.*

*At this moment in time
I appeal to your beauty & grace;*

(state your request)

*for the love of our God
reflects in your face.*

*My gratitude to you will be
filled with deference and love;*

*for the miracle you grant
will be blessed from above.*

*My request is truly just
so my enemies please do smite;*

*I will then honor your deeds
with a prayer to YOU each and every
night.*

Saint Barbara
(Patron Saint of EOD)

<u>What is a patron saint?</u>

Patron saints are selected as special protectors and guardians for certain important parts of life. These parts might include professions, diseases, buildings (for example churches), places (for example countries or cities) or events, everything that is important to humans.

Early documents show that people and churches were named after apostles and martyrs as early as in the 4th century. In recent years the pope has appointed patron saints, but any person or organization might choose one. Patron saints are usually selected when an event in the saint's life or a certain talent or interest of the saint correspond to the activity the protection is meant to cover.

<u>Saint Barbara in history</u>

Saint Barbara was a virgin and a martyr. There are no references to Saint Barbara in written history, nor is her name found in St. Jerome's revised history of martyrs.

But still the veneration of Saint Barbara was common from the

7th century and on. It was about that time the legend about her martyrdom arose and was introduced in Symeon Metaphrastes collections. The legend was frequently used by the authors (Ado, Usuard, et al.) of the enlarged description of the history of martyrs that arose in Western Europe during the 9th century.

Before the 9th century Saint Barbara was venerated in the East as well as in

the West and was a very popular saint with the Christians. It might be that the Saint Barbara that is venerated today is a mix of the lives of two separate but closely related martyrs.

According to Symeo Metaphrastes and the Latin legend told by

Mobritus, Saint Barbara's martyrdom took place in Heliopolis, Egypt. Other, more established, sources state that Nicomedia, the capital of the kingdom of Bithynia, was where the drama took place. They place the time for the event to the early 3rd century. At this time the wealthy and powerful professed to the pre-Christian religion of Graeco-Roman. Christianity was new and mostly spread among the poor.

Nicomedia was founded in 264 BC and was the capital of the East until Constantinople took over this role. The town that, today, is resting on the ruins of Nicomedia is called Izmit (a poor town with approximately 25,000 citizens, totally dependent of Constantinople) near Turkey.

The legend of Saint Barbara

In Nicomedia, in Asia Minor, a daughter to a wealthy salesman named Dioskuros was born in 210 AD. The mother died shortly after birth.

Barbara was brought up as an only child in a much shielded environment.
Both her father and the servants adored Barbara for her intellect and her beauty. Out of shyness she kept to her self and did not take part in either social life or amusements. Barbara's choice of friends made her withdrawn from other people. Her search made her susceptible to Christianity. When she heard that bishop Origenus would arrive in Alexandria she wrote him a letter, asking to be enlightened about Christianity.

The bishop sent a lay brother to teach her the new faith. Her father, who was afraid that the Christian faith would affect his business negatively, tried in every way to convert Barbara from Christianity. He arranged wealthy and noble suitors for his daughter; he built her a palace richly ornamented with icons, all for nothing. She wanted to get married to a Christian man. Finally the father became so upset that he locked her up in the castle tower.

When the father came home from a trip he found all the icons ruined and to the two windows, in the tower where she was held, a third was added. A symbol of the Trinity. She had also ordered for a cross to be painted on the floor of the room where she was confined.

The people who had been
appointed to guard Barbara told
her father that she had been
calling for Jesus Christ and Virgin
Mary in her prayers. Furious,
Dioskurus went to his daughter.
Barbara would not listen to her
father, but instead tried to redeem
him. Now frantic, Dioskurus tried
to kill her but God answered
Barbara's prayers. He sent a flash
of lighting that opened the castle
wall and she flew towards the
mountains. The father followed
her, trying to catch her. Barbara
then flew through an opening in
the mountainside that closed
behind her, making Dioskuros fail
in his attempt to catch her. She
stayed hidden in the mountain for
a while, but when she came out
her father caught her and took her
to the prefect Maximinus
(sometimes called Maximianus).

The prefect was stunned by her beauty and pleaded for her to convert from the Christian faith. Barbara refused. She was then tortured to dissuade her from her faith.

In the night a miracle happened. The dark prison cell was beaming with heavenly light, Christ revealed himself to Barbara and said —"be patient my daughter, because I am with you". He healed her wounds and when the morning broke everyone was astounded. The torture went on and more miracles happened. Burning torches meant to scorch Barbara went out as soon as they came near her. Barbara held on to her faith in spite of the torture and the prefect finally sentenced her to death.

Dioskuros, who was alternating between rage and the desire to please his daughter, asked permission to administer the death sentence himself. He dragged Barbara to the top of a nearby mountain and decapitated her. Soon after the act he was filled with agony and fled down the mountain. On his way down the slope he was hit by a flash of lightning and died instantly. The same destiny fell upon Maximinus who had pronounced the sentence. The legend states that this was the fourth sign, which led to Barbara being considered a saint. Under the leadership of lay brother Valentinos the disciples brought her body to Nicomedia and buried her in the village church. Around 500 AD emperor Justian brought her remains to Constantinople, where Pope Leo allowed a church to be built over her new grave in the late 6th century.

<u>Why is Saint Barbara the patron saint of EOD personnel?</u>

The legend about how her slayers were destroyed by lightning resulted in her being the patron saint against lightning, fire and sudden death. When black powder was introduced to the western world she also became the patron saint against accidents due to explosions, which is a very highly regarded attribute among EOD personnel.

Saint Barbara is the patron saint of various activities and places. She is probably most commonly associated with the artillery but also military engineers, fortresses,

Syria and the Bacchi Order all
have Saint Barbara as
their patron saint. The reason the
Bacchi Order has Saint Barbara as
their patron saint is that Bellman's
ancestors' name was Barbara
Klein.

<u>Why the 4th of December?</u>

On 4th of December each year
EOD personnel and artillerymen,
around the world, gather at their
regiments and garrisons to parade
and celebrate Saint Barbara. It
happens on the 4th of December
because, according to the Graeco-
Roman calendar, that is the day on
which her father executed her by
an axe-blow to the neck.
(According to all martyr historians
in the 9th century, except Rabanus
Maurus, Saint Barbara was

executed on 16th of December).

Saint Barbara is celebrated around the world and even the former Eastern European states that abolished religion for a period recognize Saint Barbara.

Saint Barbara in Art

The legend of Saint Barbara has inspired several artists, not least the old masters. Around the world, in churches and in religious paintings are pictures of Barbara and her destiny. She is often pictured with one or more of her attributes, one is the tower with three windows, a chalice in one hand and a palm leaf in the other (the palm leaf is a symbol of martyrdom and symbolises peace). She is often placed beside a piece of ordnance and/or cannonballs.

J.P. Vecchio (1480-1528) painted one of the most famous paintings of Saint Barbara. The painting is used as an altarpiece in the church of Saint Maria Formosa in Venice. Another famous painting is placed at the Royal Museum of Fine Arts in Antwerp and was painted by Jan van Eyck in 1437. Saint Barbara might also be seen in the church of Håstad outside the town of Lund, in Sweden.

ORIENTATION

You now have basic information about *Saint Barbara.*

I would like to tell you more about her and the *Seven African Powers* in my own words. Sharing her story and spreading "the word" about *Saint Barbara* will give you many blessings.

Before I speak to you about *Saint Barbara,* I need you to know that you can be EMPOWERED by her if you believe. For, there ARE dark forces in play here on earth. We all need GOD'S grace and the protection of good forces.

I begin by telling you what I know to be true of good and evil. I believe in GOD. For the purpose of sharing my knowledge,

I will assume that you do too. First, let me tell you what I know to be true in my heart of hearts.

There is a cosmic fight for good against evil. This battle continues each moment of time. Every day both YOU and I are temped and beguiled by a multitude of choices that can turn the tide.

<u>We each have free will</u>.

<u>We have choice</u>.

Knowledge is Power. Therefore, the following information will empower you to be strong. The truth will save you.

You may now begin *Orientation.*

GOD is an entity of great magnitude. His/her infinite power is immense and immeasurable, more that either you or I could ever imagine. Know that in the world of GOD there are beings created to embrace *humanity*.

For *humanity* is God's grace.

There are guardian angels, archangels, Mother Nature, and spirits of enlightenment, Pan, Saints, and a multitude of many more. One day a most handsome angel named *Lucifer* saw his own reflection and believed himself to be princely and a God in his own right.

He approached thy GOD and said that he, *Lucifer* should be the ruler of both *heaven and earth*.

"**NO**", said God. "*Be not vain, for I created heaven and earth in my own image and humanity itself is both my heart and soul*".

Lucifer was angered and soon he began to plan an uprising on every dimension and plane that existed between heaven and earth. He had many followers and surprising as it was, a revolution to control heaven began.

GOD, with sorrow in his heart, swiftly called for the mighty seraph *Michael*; for *Michael the Archangel,* was the greatest warrior of them all.

Michael called upon *Saint Raphael* and *Saint Gabriel* to gather an army and fight beside him. Together, they gathered the forces of GOOD to wage war on the forces of EVIL, led by Lucifer. The battle seemed never-ending. Archangel Michael and GOD'S forces defeated Lucifer. GOD then banished Lucifer and all his followers form heaven. One by one, they began to fall from grace.

As they fell, they each fell with the evilness, the wickedness, the immorality, the sinfulness, and the maliciousness that was in their hearts. Each of them became engulfed in foul, vile, nasty, unpleasant, disgusting, horrible appearances and demeanors.

They landed in a barren, bleak desert. A place where they were all transformed into demons and dark forces. This was a bleak, dismal, wretched place. It was a place called Hell. *Lucifer* became the ruler and he now called himself *Satan*.

At that moment in time, *Satan* pledged to fight *GOD* for every immortal soul of every human on earth.

The forces of evil surround us each and every day. *Satan* uses temptation to persuade us and then lures us to **"make a deal"**.

This is no television show. This is a fight for your immortal soul for all of eternity.

Each of us can use all the POWER we can get. Each of us can use ALL the friends we can get both here on earth and in heaven.

I have friends in heaven that can help YOU.

I have friends in heaven that will help YOU.

GOD is very busy.

He/She deals with the problems of humanity on a daily basis. When created, we were given *"free will"*, so our problems are our own to solve.

But I'm here to tell you that we ARE NOT alone.

GOD has many helpers. His/Her closest confidants are a group of seven Saints, a group led by *Saint Barbara*. This assemblage of saints represents the power of GOOD. Saint Barbara is the leader of the group. She is the most powerful of the group.

GOD is known to have a son called *Jesus Christ*. *Jesus* works closely with the group when they work as GOD'S right hand. Most people are actually familiar with each and every saint. Each saint has a following of their own right here on earth. Their names are as follows:

The Seven African Powers

Saint Barbara
Saint Francis
John the Baptist
Saint Anthony
Virgin of Mercy - Virgin Mary
Virgin of Regla - Virgin Mary
Virgin of Cobre - Virgin Mary
&
Jesus Christ

When they work together in this grouping they are called *The Seven African Powers.* Every saint, including *Saint Barbara* goes by a different name. Their new names reflect the force of their strength. Each saint as a member of the group heads a "house" which consists of their followers. These are people who acknowledge thes saints as members of *The Seven African Powers.*

The chosen people are those who become priests and priestesses. These people believe in and practice Spiritualism by relating to an individual saint. A saint whose house they then join and belong to for their entire lifetime.

Every saint chooses a #1 to represent them on earth.

This person is #1 for the saint until the day the person dies.

He/She is able to contact the saint and hear them speak. He/She is told to spread the word for good throughout the world in the name of the saint.

"I" am # 1 for Saint Barbara.

A simple example that will help you relate to this concept is that when people join a *"gang"*, they give themselves *"gang"* names, and immediately they become more powerful in the eyes of many others.

When the Saints work as *The Seven African Powers* their names change and the force of *"good"* surrounds them.

They then become a power of unbelievable might.

They become:

The Seven African Powers.

Obatala
Yemalla
Ochun
Chango
Orula
Ogum
Elegua
&
Olofi

Saint Barbara name is Chango.

Chango is the "leader" of the group.

Saint Barbara has a "trinity" as does the Father, the Son and the

Holy Ghost. She is *a young beautiful virgin girl* of 13, she is a *warrior with unlimited power and strength* and she is a *holy elderly mother* for all.

As the leader of the *Seven African Powers, Chango* is the saint of lightening and thunder. She rides a stallion with a chalice and a sword by her side. (Think of the television show - Xena, Warrior Princess, and you'll have a image to refer to).

When you hear thunder, you are hearing the sound of her steed riding into battle for someone.

When you see lightening, you are seeing the "striking" of her sword to defeat someone's foe. This, my friend, she can do for you; if YOU just believe.

BACK TO REALITY

I guess at this moment you must be thinking that I gave you more information than you need to know.

Consider yourself "*indoctrinated*".

Laura and I could not stop talking about the *Saints* on our drive home from John's house. I was excited. I was curious. I was overloaded with information, as you are now. I was also wondering if what John had told us could actually be true.

When I returned to work on Monday, I anxiously awaited John's arrival. He stopped by for coffee break and I asked him as many questions as I could about *Saint Barbara.*

This may sound silly now, but I wanted to know if I could get to know her.

Would she allow that?

Would she like me?

Would she help me?

Thinking back, I actually feel sorry for John. He must have regretted inviting me to his home and sharing his beliefs with me. I asked him every question I could think of and he patiently answered all of them to my satisfaction.

I ended my conversation by asking him how he knew that I was open to talking about this type of faith. I mean, just think about it. Here he was, a young professional starting a new job.

Then, soon after he befriended the Office Manager, he told her about *Saints* and invited her to his home to work the *Ouija Board* with him.

John said it was easy. *Saint Barbara* had told him to share the knowledge with me. He said that when he first met me he saw my *"guardian"* standing beside me and she smiled at him.

What?

What?

What did he just say?

Guardian?

What *Guardian?*

"Explain please", I begged him to tell me more?

What are you talking about?

John said that when we are born, many of us are sent to this plane of existence (*earth*) with a *guardian angel* to watch over us. He said that NOT everyone has one. Only the chosen ones blessed by GOD are sent with these protectors.

John said that most of us live our lives not even knowing that an angel walks beside us. We are preoccupied with daily happenings and immersed in stress. We can never even see beyond what is truly in front of us.

When he first met me he saw my "guardian" standing

beside me. She is an *Egyptian princess* and her name is *Odofi*.

At once, he knew that he and I had a connection. It would only take a bit of time until I would know it too. I was really excited to know this. To think that for my entire life I was never alone was just amazing to me. To know that GOD sent a protector to stand beside me and guide me through life was almost too much for me to handle.

I asked why everyone did not have a *guardian?*

Can I meet *Odofi?*

Will she talk to me?

John said something that I still contemplate to this day.

He said;

"There are many different levels of humanity".

It took many years for me to fully understand the meaning of that comment. If you accept the theory that our immortal soul returns to this plane of existence, over and over again; you know that each time we complete our lifetime we grow and then our soul becomes more enlightened.

That is why there are people who have an *awareness* of the "other side" and those that are NOT yet ready to accept that such things even exist.

<u>We ARE all human</u>.

But, we are NOT all equal in spirit.

During the next few months, John and I became close friends. I was comfortable with his faith and felt good about now knowing secrets that others did not. He told me how I could mediate and learn to evolve so that I may contact *Odofi*.

It was a blessing. I did exactly what John told me to do and I felt wonderful. I saw *Odofi's* reflection and I was in awe of her. She is young. She is beautiful. She was dressed in Egyptian garb. I know you won't believe this, she looked a little like me. As usual I was very excited and could not wait to tell John. When I did, I was surprised at his reaction. He acted like what I had just seen and experienced was just another walk in the park.

Well, maybe in his park, (I thought), not mine.

"Don't get so excited", he said.

"Many of the guardians are Egyptian. In the beginning of time the masses were Egyptians and many of them were royalty", he said.

Well, I didn't care.

She was the greatest.

She was MINE.

She was sent by GOD to be with me. John looked at me and smiled that smile of his. I wondered what was up.

He told me I was ready.

He told me that *Saint Barbara* charged him with the task of becoming my spiritual godfather and he was to bring me INTO the realm. I could not believe what I was hearing.

Me?

Me?

She wanted ME?

I was not a joiner.

I was a loner.

I never joined the Brownies or even joined a school Sorority.

I was honored.

But, now I wondered what it actually meant to be brought into the *"realm"*.

I had taken the first step, as you now have too. I was informed and had knowledge of who *Saint Barbara* was and knew about the *Seven African Powers*.

John told me that I needed to think long and hard about this. I needed to be very sure that I wanted to embrace the faith. I needed to understand that once I "invite" the *Saints* into my life, I CANNOT turn my back on them.

Not EVER.

Can you guess my answer?

Of course you know what my answer was. I did ponder over

this offer for the weekend. I said YES. YES. YES.

I was unsure and frightened. But, in my heart of hearts I knew that this was what I needed to do. I was honored and grateful for the opportunity and I said, YES.

There were many "rituals" that needed to be performed. I participated in all of them with appreciation and respect.

(Sorry, I am forbidden to share the rituals details with you).

From the moment I became a follower of *Saint Barbara's*, and a Spiritualist, and rewarded as her #1 on this plane of existence, I have known that I am truly blessed to be a member of humanity here on earth.

From that moment in time;

I became aware.

I became informed.

I became a healer.

I became a physic

I became empowered.

I became a POWER to be reckoned with and I knew it in every cell of my being.

<u>*I was now a daughter of Saint Barbara.*</u>

I began using my new blessings, knowledge and power each day, both at home and at work.

**RONNIE**, daughter of **Saint Barbara** – Priestess of **Chango**

I had completed all of my rituals and expected a great change in my life to occur. John told me I was being silly. He said that things will change in their own time. It seemed that on the *"other side"* there is no concept of time. Everything is in GOD'S time, and he/she does not ever wear a watch.

A few weeks later, while I was driving to work one morning, I heard my name being called. It sounded as if someone was greeting me with a *"good morning Ronnie"*. I turned away from the steering wheel to take a look. I did not see anything or anyone. The sound of the voice soon stopped. The next day, I was driving on the same route to work and again I heard a man's voice wishing me well. I quickly turned to the right, and looked at the home where the sound was coming from. All I saw was a statue of *Saint Anthony* sitting on someone's front lawn. It was the type of statue that you often see in a person's front yard. I did not see anyone standing near the statue, so I turned back, kept my eyes on the road and continued driving. A few minutes later, I heard another voice. This time it was a soft female voice telling me to have a good day.

I turned to the left to see, standing about 2 feet directly in front of me, a statue of the *Virgin Mary*. I smiled and looked away. But then something made look back at this beautiful reflection and in an instant a feeling of calm came over me and I knew. It took me a moment, but I knew that the *Saints* had been making contact with me through their images of the statues.

I not only realized what was going on, I embraced the moment. *"Good morning to YOU too, Good morning to you ALL"*, I said.

The Saints were speaking to me.

ME.

I could hardly wait to tell John. But, John was not at all surprised. Yup, it seemed that I was connecting with *Saints*. I could hear them. Every time I saw a statue or any type of image of a *Saint*, it spoke to me. For weeks I found myself having conversations with the *Saints* each and every morning on my way to work.

After a while, I knew where every statue of every *Saint* was placed on the drive to work. John said that that many more wonders awaited me. To this day, I am still able to speak to the *Saints* through their images.

On my first trip to Sedona, AZ., I visited the Chapel of the Holy Cross. This is a beautiful tourist attraction. It is a small chapel on a hillside over looking the splendor of GOD himself/herself. I walked up the hillside, through the doorway and sat down to pray. My eyes were closed when I heard someone call my name. My companions had just left to go to the gift shop and I thought they were calling for me.

My eyes remained closed and I continued to pray.

I heard my name being called again.

"Ronnie".

"Ronnie"?

It was a man's voice. It was a deep, gentle voice of someone I did not know. I opened my eyes and no one was there. I took a deep long yawn and thought I was just tired from the excitement of the trip.

Again, I heard the voice.

This time I answered.

I don't know what I was thinking, because there was no one standing there. But, I replied.

"Yes"?

"Yes"? I said.

"Who are you?

What do you want"?

"Ronnie". I heard him say, "It is I, *Saint John.* I want to wish you well. Tell John I send him my blessings".

I left the chapel engulfed in a feeling of tranquility. My friends asked me if I was okay. Without my even knowing it, I had begun to cry. A stream of tears were flowing from my eyes.

I called John as soon as I returned to the hotel.

He had heard that Sedona, AZ. was filled with vortexes. He had also known of *Saint John*. As a matter of fact, he knew him well. *Saint John* was my friend John's patron *Saint*.

John thanked me for giving him the message and he said that he was very proud of me. Though John was now my spiritual "*godfather*" he had chosen NOT to share his knowledge of how things would happen to me. I was affected differently as a "novice". I was a child learning to walk by myself. I was a child learning about my senses and experiencing how they affected me. He threw me into the darkness. He then left me alone to learn by myself.

John chose to allow me to experience every event for myself. He felt that each and every time would be a gift for me to enjoy. He did not want to ruin the surprise.

A few weeks later I was on a business trip to Manhattan. I stopped at *Saint Patrick's Cathedral* to light a few candles. This was something I did quite often. I walked down the side aisle looking for *Saint Anthony.* I had been introduced to him years before by a close friend. I always would light a candle beside him when I was in town.

As I walked the aisle, I heard a man's voice calling my name. *"Ronnie"? "Ronnie"?* I turned expecting to see someone from my Manhattan office. The only person in front of me was a homeless man, lying down on a pew, and he was sleeping. I turned around and was stunned to realize that I was standing in directly in front of the statue of *Saint John*.

"Hello, Ronnie. It's me, John".

"Don't you remember me"?

I looked directly into his eyes and replied. I began to have a conversation with this statue just as if I was talking to an old friend. He asked about me and my family. He told me to give his blessings to John and his regards to *Saint Barbara*.

I felt elated. I felt great. Then I turned around and saw a

couple looking straight at me. They were both grinning. They had not actually heard my conversation. But, they certainly <u>did</u> see me talking to my new friend as if he was a real person.

Oh well, I didn't care.

I had a secret.

I was learning that there was so much more to life than I knew before. I was making friends from the *"other side"*. The *Saints* themselves were taking me into their fold.

I had prayer cards of *Saint Barbara* and I light candles to her each night. John and I spoke about spiritual things each and every day. He said it was OUR job to fight for good against evil each and every day. He said it was up to us to help humanity. I thought to myself, who does he think I am, *Xena – Warrior Princess?*

On my next visit to John's house, he told me he had a present for me. It was a surprise. It was a gift that I needed and he was sure that I would want it. My friend, Margo, had joined me on that day.

We were both really curious.

John walked me into the room he had set up as an altar. This was where he did the rituals. This was where he did healings and readings. This was where he helped humanity. I had walked in with my eyes closed.

John said, *"Open your eyes"*.

There, standing in front of me, staring me right in the eye was a FOUR FOOT statue of *Saint Barbara.*

It was truly amazing. She is truly beautiful. Her image is on the front cover of this book.

The statue was something that you would see in a church. I'm a short woman and she was almost as tall as I was. John had her standing on a pedestal.

I was in awe.

I was speechless.

This is my gift to you *"Goddaughter"*, he said.

He said that having her would make it easier for me to

practice the faith. I set her up in my bedroom. I keep her close by my side while I sleep for guidance and protection. I am a daughter of *Saint Barbara*. I am a priestess of *Chango*. I am *"open"* to the forces of the *"other side"* I must be aware and on guard at all times.

At work, I did not immediately share details of my new faith. I began to practice it by bringing flowers into my office and keeping a glass of water on my desk. It was not that I was embarrassed to tell anyone. It was because I wasn't sure how to tell anyone.

One by one, people would ask me about the water and about the flowers. When that happened, I would share just a "bit" of information. Everyone, I really mean everyone, was always amazed and wanted to learn more.

Soon, I began sharing my new life with people I trusted with the information. A group of employees became my confidants and we began to walk the path of enlightenment together.

I healed the sick.

I gave guidance to those that lost their way.

I began doing so much for so many that I was physically ill. When John saw that I looked physically drained, he asked me about details of what I had been doing regarding helping people by using the faith. He immediately reprimanded me. I had been doing too much. Too much without being paid. I didn't understand. I wanted to help people. I wanted to share what I now knew to be true. I didn't need money. I didn't want money.

But, John explained to me that nothing in life is free. Everyone has to *pay the piper*. He said that the price could be a minimum amount, but everyone must pay. From that moment on I asked for and received payment every time I gave my help. Every time I spent the money on flowers and candles for Saint Barbara.

I was wearing myself out. But I truly enjoyed practicing my new faith and seeing the powerful results I was getting.

People began to gravitate towards me. I was the Office Manager and employee traffic was common in my private office. But one day a young woman entered and asked for my help. She said that her Supervisor sent her. They were told that "I" was the one she should see about her problem.

She was a technical employee and I did not supervise her directly. I knew her Supervisor and I knew that she was a Claims Representative. I thought she had a problem with a claim, or with one of my staff or with the office workplace.

I invited her to sit down.

She seemed a bit nervous.

She bowed her head down and started to speak.

It seems that her husband and she had been trying to have a baby for over nine years. Nothing and no one had been able to help them conceive.

"Would YOU help us", she asked. I think I bit my tongue, I was so surprised.

I guess there were many "believers" in the office. The word about me had spread. The needy were walking through my doorway and asking for my help. I'm not a fertility doctor. I'm not a midwife. I'm just a believer. But, I am someone who is in close association with the *Powers that Be*. I knew that I could help her. But, would I be allowed to help?

I told her I would need permission to help her.

I told her that I would speak to *Saint Barbara* about her plight and I would get back to her soon.

Saint Barbara did give me permission to help her.

I was told by *Saint Barbara* that I would have to call upon more than one member of the *Seven African Powers* to help her. I was given permission to explain this to her. I would have to identify the saints to her by the names they use in the realm.

She would then have to do exactly as I said.

She would have to believe in them and give them all offerings.

She would have to use the power of the healing stone.

She would have to pray.

She would have to *BELIEVE.*

This she did religiously for 4 months. After 4 months she came into my office one morning and began to cry. She told me that she saw her doctor and was pregnant.

Her child was a gift *from Obatala and Ochun.*

<u>These *Saints* were sent to help her by *Saint Barbara.*</u>

Her son is destined for greatness. He is a gift from GOD. He is an example of the power of goodness. He was presented to her from the right hand of GOD.

<u>*Saint Barbara*</u> is part of me now and forever.

I was taught that if I was ever in need to simply call out her name. If you remember from the legend I shared with you earlier in this book, she was killed by her father. It is said that GOD wanted the child beauty to be safe in heaven for eternity. When she called out to be saved, GOD made her a promise.

GOD said that if a member of humanity ever called out the name of *Saint Barbara* in time of need, they will be saved.

One day at work, I wasn't feeling very good. I was definitely coming down with something. Everything was going wrong. An minor annoyance became a big big problem that day. A vendor had been trespassing in our office at night. He/she was leaving flyers with sales items listed. Of course, employees were calling in many orders to be delivered at work.

I took a flyer and called the phone number listed. I then complained to them about their unauthorized night visits and advised them that I was about to call the police. I finished the phone call and contacted the police department. At that moment I thought the situation had come to an end.

The security of the office workplace was always a priority concern of mine. I was proud to have a safe and secure work environment for the employees.

It was a beautiful summer day and most of the staff was out for lunch. I received a call from the Receptionist. I was told that there was a young man in the Reception Area with a wagon full of packages and was going into the office to distribute them. I told her to stop him and I rushed to the area immediately.

Standing there in front of me was a man in his twenties wheeling a wagon with approximately 50 packages. He abruptly informed me that he was going into the office and I could not stop him.

I told him that I had called his company and that I already called the police.

During our conversation, another young man, who was also in his twenties, entered the Reception Area. He was wearing a t-shirt and shorts. He asked to see a sales representative and then he sat down. He was a policyholder visiting to discuss his Automobile policy.

He of course overheard the conversation I was having.

The vendor told me that he wanted to see the "boss". I told him that "I" was the boss. I know I sounded weak, but I truly wasn't feeling well. The male employees who worked directly for me were out to lunch. The vendor smirked at me and started walking from the Reception Area into the employees work area.

I told the Receptionist to call Building Security.

I again told the vendor to leave. His appearance and demeanor were a little bit frightening to me, and I guess he sensed that I was just a little bit overwhelmed.

At that moment I realized I had lost control.

I closed my eyes for a second and I prayed.

"Saint Barbara, please hear my plea".

"I need your help".

"Protect me – Save me".

As I opened my eyes, I saw the young policyholder stand up

and walk towards us. He reached into his pocket and pulled out his wallet. He flipped it open, showed us a badge and said in an authoritative tone.

"**POLICE** Miss, do you need my help"?

He then turned to the vendor and said, "The lady told you to leave the premises. Leave right now".

He walked to the front door of our office suite and directed the rude young man out.

In less than a minute, Building Security arrived and then the male employees who worked directly for me returned from lunch. I thanked the police officer repeatedly and gave him every

Company "handout" that the Sales Department had available.

I had called out for help and SHE, my savior, my mother, sent the cavalry.

SHE has never let me down.

I feel her in my heart.

I feel her in my soul.

I know that she will be with me forever.

If I die an old woman, SHE will be waiting for me with her steed by her side. She will help me mount her stallion.

Together, she and I will journey to heaven.

Invitation To A "MASS"

The months passed by quickly. John and I had become best friends and of course we had issues, as do all good friends. It was obvious to both of us that we had a spiritual connection. At night if I meditated and focused on John, I could connect with him while I slept. He would answer me while I was in a REM state. The next day we would recap the conversation we had during the night. We were always both right on target. This I thought was cool. That is until John told me to stop. He said that I was interrupting his sleep too much.

I called our sleep connection my private *"1-800-Call John"* number.

We also had a private joke about John being younger than me. We decided that I was sent to earth first so I could clear the way for John and get settled in while I waited for him. He and I were supposed to join humanity at the same time. But, when he was told to start his journey and be born, John should have, could have and certainly "would have" delayed the process by telling every single energy force, including GOD, what he thought they could be doing better.

Yup, that's my godfather. He had a habit of involving himself in everything he felt he could help make better.

I was totally ready to try everything spiritual I had ever heard of. It was almost as if I was addicted to the new "knowledge and power" I had been given.

John and I disagreed on how quickly I should progress into the realm and how I should proceed with my learnings. I felt I was ready for anything now, right NOW. John said I was a novice and on the other side, I would be considered a new born that still needed guidance and protection.

I knew I was evolving and I felt my newfound power changed me. I was doing healings and readings for people. I was doing good and I had positive results. I was helping people. I was giving so much of myself that I started getting headaches every time I did something spiritual.

I was in daily contact with *Saint Barbara* and the other Saints I had been introduced to. *Saint Barbara* was proud of me. John said that she chose me to join her fold. He said, she wanted me to accept her love and devotion and be her # 1.

What?

What did he say?

I really had to contemplate this request. After some time I knew in my heart of hearts that this was something that I was destined to do.

It may sound unreal to you. You may ask what in the world was expected of me. I was told to live a life helping others and begin spreading the name of *Saint Barbara* with deference and love.

This I have always done.

This book will spread her name throughout the world.

World, may I introduce you all to the mother of my soul? I introduce you all to **Saint Barbara virgin and martyr.**

One day I was watching a television show about a housewife who said that she could channel a being from the other side. She had a following which included many celebrities. I watched and saw a film of her speaking in different tongues. People were flocking to her session by the hundreds. She was advising the world of what was to come. She was making mucho money doing this. I was very interested and really impressed.

Before the show had ended John called me. I answered and sensed his upset immediately. He was deeply concerned and spoke in an angry, loud tone.

He asked if I was watching the show. He had been watching the exact same television show that I was. He said that this woman was trouble and that "we" had to do something about it.

What?

What did he say?

John said that as he looked at the television screen and that as he watched the pretty blonde housewife "channel" a being from the other side, he saw EVIL. He said that she was channeling a consort of Lucifer himself.

I took a deep breath. I could not believe what I was hearing. Not that I did not believe in John; I certainly did believe in him. Not because I did not know that there was EVIL here on earth; I certainly did know. It was that he used the word **WE**, <u>**WE**</u> had to do something about it.

"John, I am a short, chubby, middle-aged lady, sitting here eating ice-cream watching TV. I've never lifted my hand in anger to anyone other than my sister when we were kids. I am a novice in the realm. I've never fought for good against evil. This woman lives on the West Coast. She is a multi-millionaire and has hundreds of followers. I am

NOT the television persona Xena, Warrior princess.

<u>*What in the world do you expect ME to do*</u>"?

"Ronnie, he said get real. You have to understand that we live with negative energies in our lives everyday".

YOU have to be aware when evil shows itself.

YOU have to be *good.*

YOU have to do *good.*

YOU have to spread the word for good when evil speaks.

This YOU must do each and every day for the rest of your life".

Well, I thought, he's not asking much of me?

Is he?

I sort of redirected the conversation away from his comments. I said, "But she can channel a spirit. She can speak for a being who comes from, from who knows where?

"So can I", he said.

What?

What?

What did he just say?

I asked him to repeat himself. I asked him if he meant that he actually has had a spirit speak "through" him. A spirit who actually spoke right through his mouth?

Yup, that was what he meant.

I could not believe what I was hearing. I asked him why had he not he told me. His answer was typical John. He said *"all in good time Turbane – all in good time"*.

This type of comment always bothered me. John was younger than me. He may have more time here on earth then me. I needed to know now, <u>right now</u>!

The next day at work I told Laura all about what John said.

We approached him and asked questions about channeling.

We asked for more information.

"Please, please, we begged him, please tell us". We wanted to know it all. We needed to know everything.

John explained that it was common for energies from the other side to contact people. Many people have no concept of what is happening to them at that time. Everyone has the ability to open their minds eye and have energy enter their essence and touch their soul. If not protected, negative forces attach themselves to savor "life" as we know it. This is commonly called possession.

Is seems that "channeling" was something that John had experienced often throughout his life. He would join a group of his trusted friends and a ritual would begin. They would protect themselves and welcome only positive forces from the other side. Then entities would take over the body of one of the group and information would be shared with all.

This meeting is properly called a *MASS*. The public refers to it a *Séance*.

As always, Laura and I could not contain ourselves. Laura said that she too was a true believer. She too respected *Saint Barbara*.

Laura invited us over for dinner at her house. She also invited two other friends, Gladys and Sara, to join us. They agreed to join us for dinner and a Mass.

The night scheduled for the dinner finally came. We rushed through the meal and sat there staring at John, waiting and wondering what was going to happen.

First he explained what was going to happen so we would not be frightened.

Second, he set the stage by placing ritual items that he brought with him on the dining room table.

Third, he did a ritual to protect us for the MASS.

He told us not to be scared.

We would have to hold hands and close our eyes if we wanted to. Most of all we needed to "believe" in what we were doing. We needed to trust in John.

We would start once we had the permission and protection of *Saint Barbara*. She would watch over us during the evening. We would have to be patient and wait to see who would "come through" the doorway that we were opening. We would also have to be patient because "we" could not STOP the MASS until the last entity coming through would say to us that they were the last one in wait.

Okey, Dokey.

You think you're confused. I was in total shock. We waited and we waited and we waited some more. We were all frightened and a little scared. We had dimmed the lights so as to not use too much energy in the room.

This was like right out of the movies. I was actually at a *Séance*.

Oops.

I mean MASS.

Then it happened. John started to moan. I looked at him and he looked different. He had a funny grin on his face. He rolled up his shirt sleeves. He rolled up his pants. He sat down on the floor. He looked at cach of us and said.

"Ladies, join me".

His voice was different.

He was <u>NOT John</u>.

He had an accent.

His demeanor had changed.

I asked who he was.

He said, "my name is "Como Quero".

"Como Quero, great Haitian king and husband of many hundreds of wives.

Ladies, come.

Come, please come and join me".

John then extended his hand to us. I still don't believe it really happened. I still don't believe how we all reacted. One by one, we walked over to him and sat beside him. There we were four women sitting in a circle totally memorized by this entity who had taken over control of John's body.

We really enjoyed this time. We acted as if we just made a new friend. *Como* spoke to us about life, past and present. He spoke about his wives and he spoke of how we should live our lives. All of a sudden it dawned on me that it was a long time since this man I was looking at spoke and acted like he was John.

I stared directly at him and said, "John, are you alright?" The face I looked into looked back at me and said;

"*Body in trouble, body in trouble*."

Before we started, John told me what to do if something went wrong. At the time I thought he was nuts. I was nervous, but I remembered what he told me to do. I followed what were previous instructions. The man looked back at me and said, *"Hurry, hurry, body in trouble."*

Again, I did what John had told me to do. I guess I did not do it right the first time. In an instant John started to moan and groan and started talking in his own voice. He told us he had a terrible headache and needed to lie down for a while. We got him aspirin, a cool cloth for his forehead and helped him to the couch.

It seemed that over an hour had passed. John had "channeled" the entity we now knew as *Como Quero* for way too long.

The experience was taking a toll on John. This event changed my perception of all things.

For many months after, our group would meet at Laura's house and have MASS after MASS. It gave us a very powerful feeling.

We knew things that most of humanity could not even comprehend.

I had made a new friend.

He was a great Haitian king.

He was the husband to many hundreds of wives.

We called him *Como.*

To the spiritual world and to a world of believers he was known as the great Haitian king:

<u>*Como Quero.*</u>

IF HE CAN – I CAN TOO

In the following months, I was getting stronger each and every day. Even John said he could not believe what I was experiencing and how "open" spiritually I had become.

I was taking it upon myself to spread the word about *Saint Barbara.*

I began doing readings, rituals, healings and counseling for people often. I began charging them and thcy happily paid to receive my help.

At work if you knew what was actually happening, then you would notice many and I mean many employees had glasses of *water* on their desks. These were people who wanted to take the first step towards enlightenment and walk the path with ME.

I had a group of followers at work. Often, during lunchtimes we would talk about our spiritual journey. Women always wanted to know how to attract love and happiness. Men always wanted to attract wealth and power.

One day, a manager who I had a good relationship with shared a personal family problem with me. He was quite distraught. It seems that I had walked into his office at the moment he ended a conversation with his wife about his teenage daughter. They were concerned that she was not sleeping and her school grades were falling down. She had told them that she was having dreams about her dead grandmother.

Her grandmother was reaching out to her and asking for help. The daughter was not as frightened as she was tired. She had loved her grandmother very much. They had a close relationship. But, she had not slept for days and it was affecting her deeply.

My friend and his wife were worried. They were taking their daughter to the doctor the next day. They had thought she might have a serious health condition.

Though I wasn't sure exactly what his belief system was, I just had to offer my help to my friend for his daughter. I knew he was open-minded. I knew he liked me and would not laugh at my offer to help his family in a spiritual way.

I told him I was involved in the practice of healing and that I also was in contact with the saints. I asked him if he would like me to talk to them about this situation.

He said YES, definitely YES. What actually surprised me was not his answer; it was his immediate acceptance of my offer to help his family.

I've learned that people will embrace the "unbelievable" if they are in crisis or feel a sense of fear and hopelessness.

That very night, I stood in front of my altar and I looked

directly into the eyes of my statue of *Saint Barbara.*

I told her of my friend's plight and asked if I had permission to help him. She said YES. Now, there are two points I need you to know.

First, a person must "want" my help for me to be able to help them.

Second, I must have the permission of *Saint Barbara* before I am able to work my magic.

She told me what to ask my friend about and how to respond to him once I received the answers. She of course knew immediately what the situation was all about.

The next day I stopped by my friend's office. I asked how the situation was and he said that it was the same. I then said that I was given permission to help him and I needed to ask him some questions about his family. He felt there was no problem with this and told me to ask away. I asked the questions that I was told to ask. They were as follows:

1- When did your mother die?

2- What was the relationship between your mother and your daughter like?

3- Is your mother's funeral process totally over?

4- Is there anything left for your family to do for your mother?

He looked at me in shock.

He said, "Why did you ask that? How did you know about that?" He told me that he and his brother had been so busy that on more that one occasion they delayed making the purchase of a "gravestone" for his mother.

He told me that just a few weeks earlier, he spoke to his brother and insisted that they both travel to where their mother was buried and handle this matter. It was way overdue and he had started to feel a little guilt. But, he knew I would understand, other things were taking priority in their lives. I of course knew exactly what was going on and I knew that I needed to tell him in a forthright and honest way. I needed to tell him immediately so that his daughter would start to sleep at night and go back to living the normal life of a teenager.

"Okay, (I said), listen to me carefully so that you will understand the importance of what I tell you. Regardless of what you think or believe, you MUST do what I tell you to do."

He looked at me and immediately nodded yes. I explained to him that when a person passes on they leave this earth and cross over in their own time. Each soul must complete their unfinished business here on earth before they are able to leave for the "other side".

It can be as simple as having a spirit say their good-byes to their loved ones. It could be as involved as a soul not leaving until THEY decide that everything is in order and that they may now move on. After hearing the answers to my questions I told him the following:

Because your mother and your daughter had a close loving relationship, she was the one who was "open" enough to hear your mother's plea.

Your mother wants a headstone NOW. She needs it to bring closure to her life on earth. It will enable her to move on. Both you and your brother should be ashamed of yourself for not bringing this process to an end for your whole family. You must purchase the stone and have it placed immediately. Offer her your love and apologies and she will forgive you.

He looked at me and smiled.

He told me I must be right. It seemed that his daughter started having these visitations from her grandmother right after he and his brother delayed buying the headstone. He said he would call his brother immediately and take care of the situation ASAP.

I left his office feeling very good about myself and about the fact that I helped a friend in need.

I did not talk about it anymore to him. I didn't want to embarrass him. Though, a few weeks later, I did ask how his daughter was feeling. He said, "Fine, everything is just fine". He smiled at me and I smiled back at him. We both knew what had happened for his family to get back to "FINE".

Boy was I feeling proud of myself. I thought I no longer needed John for advice or approval of what I was doing spiritually. I had begun doing things on my own and it felt great.

John was moving up the ladder of success quickly. He left our workplace and accepted a great job offer from an insured who was impressed with John's work performance.

We remained close and spoke to each other each day.

The girls and I continued to talk about the "masses" we had

with John and often spoke of our new friend *"Como Quero"*.

A few weeks had passed and John and I had a parting of the ways. I truly don't remember how the disagreement started or what the details of our disagreement were all about. What I do remember is that it was a whopper.

He told me to *"burn I hell"* and I said, *"Same to you buddy"*.

I know you don't believe me, but you can even ask John. I know he won't remember either. It seems that "time" dims the memory.

That I've learned is a gift from GOD.

So, there I was, empowered and feeling that I could do anything that I wanted to do.

What the girls and I missed most was having a Mass.

What I wanted to do was to have a Mass and see my new friend.

What I decided was that if John could oversee a Mass, so could I.

<u>If he could do it, so could I.</u>

HELP, I NEED HELP!

Laura invited the girls and me over to her house for dinner.

We were all very excited.

I decided to give a MASS a try without John being part of it. The girls convinced me that I was as strong if not stronger than John. They all said they would help me through it. We had all been part of Masses before and together I thought that we would be invincible.

Though I had not spoken to John for weeks, Laura had kept in touch with him. I was missing him each and every day. I knew he was busy at his new job and that his life was on the fast track. John was very busy. So in my own mind I convinced myself that his friendship was meant to be a passing phase for me. It was meant to be used as the introduction; a means for me to meet *Saint Barbara*.

I was at a point in my life that I accepted everything as it came to me.

The night came quickly. We were all very excited. We ate dinner at the dining room table and quickly cleaned it off to prepare for the Mass.

We prepared very slowly.

The girls and I remembered every single thing that John did when he controlled the Mass.

We dimmed the lights.

I tried not to be, but I was really nervous and a bit scared. As I started the process Sarah said she saw my face changing into the face of an old woman's.

I did not stop.

I continued with what I thought was the proper process.

I opened the doorway to the *"other side"*.

Then I protected us all from dark forces and negative energies.

I invited only positive forces from the other side to join us.

Sarah said, *"Do you hear that"*? She heard a tinkling, jingling sound. No one else did. So, I continued with the Mass.

At that moment Gladys screamed.

"STOP"!

"STOP RIGHT NOW"!

I stopped the session and we calmed Gladys down. When we asked what had happened she explained the following.

She saw the back door of the dining room fly open and the great spirit of *Ocoo*, (I'll explain who *Ocoo* is in a moment) demanded that we stop the session immediately. Gladys said she felt fear, started to sweat and knew instantly that *Ocoo* had connected with her to **"save us"**.

I ended the session ASAP and we all left Laura's house.

It was late and I was really drained. I got home, took a bath and started to prepare my clothes for the next workday.

When I emptied my purse to change it for a different one I put my hand in the bottom and felt something unfamiliar. I reached in and reached out with a set of KEYS. I thought, what in the world is this?

Whose keys are these?

Where did they come from?

I got really nervous and immediately called Laura. I told her what had just happened to me. Laura was silent. She then began to tell me that after we all left she started to clean up. She also was planning her dress for the next day but stopped when she could not find her keys. She was going to put her car in the garage and got nervous because she thought her keys were lost.

We both knew that was silly, because her car was in the front of her house and she needed the car keys to drive home. She retraced her steps and the last place she remembered seeing the keys were in her bedroom. She had come home that night and placed them on her nightstand next to her bed.

I described the keys that I found in my purse to Laura. She said; *"Oh my GOD. Oh dear GOD what is going on with us tonight"*?

<u>I had Laura's keys.</u>

I told Laura not to worry. I told her that we would figure everything out tomorrow. All the girls and I would get together and we WOULD figure out everything. Laura was okay with that because she had a spare set of keys and I would be returning her set to her the next day.

Of course I did not sleep at all. I was really worried because I did not have a clue what had happened.

I arrived at work and Laura, Sarah and Gladys were all waiting for me in my office. Laura had told them what happened.

I gave Laura her keys back. I would now like to tell you who the great spirit of *Ocoo* is. When John began the Masses at Laura's he was quite surprised how easily the Masses began and how quickly spirits came through to speak to us. The first spirit to come through to us at our first Mass at Laura's house was *Ocoo*.

Laura was married and had one son. She had spent her entire adult life in the house that we were now having the Masses in.

Laura's marriage was an unhappy one and she had lived through a gambit of negative emotions throughout the years. But, she always felt safe in her home and never wanted to leave.

Laura's home is in a Long Island, N.Y. town that is known to be a historical "*Indian*" homeland.

It is a very spiritual place.

I believe that the lot her house was built on is <u>*Sacred Indian burial ground*</u>.

John met *Ocoo* at our first Mass. It seems that *Ocoo* has watched over Laura since she was a young married woman. She never knew his spirit was there. She did however feel a presence and sensed love and protection when she was in her home alone.

This was and is one of the sweetest true love stories for the century. This showed us that two dimensions can overlap and that LOVE can reach out over time and space.

Ocoo had loved Laura throughout her adult life. Laura was now returning his feelings. She was falling in love with *Ocoo*.

As a young married woman she lived in a loveless marriage in this house. Now as a widow she found a love that was never-ending. She embraced it fully.

John introduced us all to *Ocoo* early in our sessions. His spirit visited us each time we had a Mass. He gave us his blessings. He also gave Laura a great feeling of love and comfort. This was a great gift to Laura.

This is why, when Gladys said she saw the figure of an Indian warrior standing in the doorway demanding that we stop the Mass immediately, we all knew that we must stop.

We must stop immediately.

<u>OCOO</u> told us to.

There we were, four middle aged women who knew that we had bit off a little more than we could chew.

Okay, I will take full responsibility. I thought I knew what I was doing. I guess I didn't.

Laura said, "I think we better call John for help".

I said "NO".

They looked at me and asked if I knew what had happened and asked what I was going to do about it? What if the Mass was going to cause trouble?

Okey, dokey, they were right. I guess I made a boo-boo and I needed John's help too.

We all knew we needed John's help. But, I wasn't going to be the one to call him. He told me to burn in hell.

Laura called John that very same day. We finally made contact with him. It was in the afternoon. He said he wasn't feeling well. It seems the night before he was out-of-state for a business meeting. At night his associates and he went out to dinner and John got violently ill. He actually, (excuse me for saying this), pooped in his pants. He went to his hotel immediately.

Laura offered her sympathy and knew right away that John's illness happened at the same time that I had screwed up our Mass. Now she had to tell John about it.

"What"?

"What"!

"Who the hell did she let in"?

John was angry.

John was furious.

John wanted to kill me.

He told Laura that he had to think this situation over and he would call me back.

Laura told us all what John had said. I knew what he meant when he asked who I let in. He meant that I opened the doorway to the *"other side"* and did not fully protect us. He meant that I allowed some negative spirit, being

Force, entity or energy through and it attached themselves to us.

Okey, dokey, I admit it. I made a boo-boo. Okay, so I made a mistake. Enough already, I know it, I screw up big time.

I was totally confused. I began imagining the worst. I asked myself so many questions.

Did I personally change the destiny of the world?

Can John fix this for us?

Does *Saint Barbara* hate me?

Did I misuse my power for good and mistakenly help evil?

Help John. Please help.

Before the work day ended I received a call from John. He was calm and spoke to me slowly. I knew he was really mad at me, his voice had an abrupt tone to it and he spoke to me as if I were a stranger.

He asked questions and I answered. He wanted to know exactly how I started the Mass and how I protected us during the Mass. What rituals did I use?

I told him everything I knew. He then asked me something weird. He asked if any of us, especially me, had recently been involved with or close to a "death". Had someone close died? Hmmmmmmmmmm?

The girls said no.

I thought for a moment and said yes. Then he told me to tell him in detail everything that I experienced since we parted ways.

When we were friends John and I knew everything that happened to each other every single day. But since we had not spoken for a few months there was a void. He needed to fill that void and update himself about what I had been doing spiritually.

When I accepted the realm, when I accepted John as my Godfather, it was forever. Regardless of our foolish parting, we were and will always be linked together, forever.

He told me to tell him everything and that I should speak slowly. He was taking notes.

I told him about Laura's keys, the sounds that Sarah heard and that she saw my face turn into an old woman. I told him that Gladys saw *Ocoo* and then I told him what I tell you now.

I have a close friend Kendall. I've known her for a lifetime and John had met her too. We all worked for the same employer when I first met John.

Kendall's mother was very ill. When I had visited her in the hospital she was in a coma. I sat in her hospital room alone for a moment when I heard a voice. I looked at the mother and she was sleeping. But, as I looked at her I heard her voice speaking directly at me. She said, "Ronnie, stay Kendall's friend. She's a good girl, stay close to her."

I had never told anyone about this. A few days later I visited Kendall at home while her mom was still in the hospital. I was in the kitchen alone and I heard a man's voice saying, *"Leave this house now"*. I looked around and saw no one. Again I heard the voice. This time he used my name and said, *"Ronnie, leave now"*.

I looked around again and this time I noticed a cross with the image of *Jesus Christ* hanging on the kitchen wall.

He was speaking to me. I left and walked outside. A few days after that Kendall's mother passed away. I went with my friend Margo to the funeral parlor and we sat in the back. As I sat there, I heard a woman's voice calling out to me.

I asked Margo if she heard anything, she said no. Margo then walked outside and I was sitting alone. Again, I heard the voice calling me, it said, *"Ronnie, Ronnie, come up here to me"*. I looked up and saw the casket placed in the front of the room. It was an open casket and the mother was lying in it waiting to be seen by all.

I wasn't afraid.

I walked up to the casket, looked directly at her body and heard her speak to me. She said,

"Isn't this just lovely? Look at the material. Kendall is such a good girl. I will stay close to make sure she is okay. Remain her friend Ronnie, stay close to her".

I said okay and left.

I told Margo what had happened. She did not laugh or seem surprised. She seemed to understand and said not to worry. She said the mother would rest in peace. We both went to the funeral. I sat in the church when I heard the mother call out to me. The coffin was closed, but I still heard her voice. Margo said she was feeling something also. She told me to pray for the mother. Margo walked up to the coffin. I did not. I heard her speak and I told her to Rest in Peace.

This I told John. He sighed and said he now understood. He told me that I was NOT to be close to death in my first year of spiritualism. He said I was OPEN to *contact* and still a novice on the other side. He said if I play with fire that I would get burned.

John told me that there were rituals that I should have done before I got close to death. He said that I was warned in Kendall's house that death was close. He said that because I was who I was, her mother had made contact with me. She might be involved with what happened the other night.

John said that I allowed a poltergeist to cross over and that they were playing with us by moving the keys from Laura's room and putting them in my purse. Sarah had always been open to this type of thing and it was she who heard the keys jingle and saw a dark image move behind me towards my purse sitting on the couch. He said there might be forces in play here.

John said that it was my fault for starting something I could not finish. He said it was my fault that he got sick the night before. It seems that because of our spiritual connection he picked up on the event and it had affected him physically in a negative way. He said that the same group of people would have to meet again at the same time; in the same place and that HE would have to do an exorcism.

I could not believe what I was hearing. I saw those movies and they were too much for me to handle. I felt like I was living in one of them now.

I said okay. I would plan it. I told John that he shared in the blame. He NEVER told me any of this. Why didn't he warn me?

When I accepted the "realm" in my life forever, John accepted being part of my life forever.

We both new that whatever our differences were, we needed each other. From that moment on we have never, ever walked different paths. We have been together in mind and spirit for over 25 years now.

Now, let's get back to the girls. The girls were waiting for me patiently and they all agreed to again meet at Laura's house to solve this mystery. Laura was actually pleased to have us back to visit and she felt great comfort that *Ocoo* saved us all.

We had dinner and we started. It was scary.

Not totally, but it was a lot like what you see in the movies.

John had brought everything that he needed for the ritual of *banishment*. First, he banished the poltergeist from the house. It seems that this was a young spirit, one that had recently crossed over. John said we were lucky that it had crossed over recently and that he was able to banish the soul. If a stronger force had crossed over through the doorway that I had opened, we would have been in "*deep shit*". Even John might not have been able to handle the situation without asking for help.

Next, we needed to find out if any other entity or force was in the house and if it had attached itself to any of us.

There was.

IT did.

It seems that the spirit of Kendall's mother attached herself to ME at the funeral parlor. I did not protect myself before I entered a house filled with souls that had recently crossed over.

John explained that at this time he could control and would remove her attachment to me.

He performed a ritual and said I was now safe. He explained though that he could not send her to the other side. Each soul decides when to "move on". It's when they take care of any unfinished business that they may have. So, I was free of Kendall's mom. But, was she gone forever?

WHAT I'VE LEARNED

The years passed slowly, as they always have for me. John and I still remain close and I've had many more encounters that are unexplainable to this day.

I have helped people by phone, in person, by e-mail and by letter. My feedback is always accurate and I'm pleased to say that I've helped many individuals.

I have spread the word about *Saint Barbara* and have learned more about her background and testimonials by doing research myself. Did you know that the town of *Santa Barbara*, CA. was named after her?

Did you know that she is the Patron Saint of artillery men and during the Viet Nam war her image was placed on a hilltop which was fought over? This was the <u>only</u> hilltop in the country that had NO causalities during the war.

Did you know that a statue of *Saint Barbara* stands proudly in a Vanderbilt mansion in Newport, Rhode Island? When you enter the main hall take a moment and look around. You will see *Barbara.*

You can learn about her in your library or on the Internet. You will be in awe and amazed at what you will find out about her.

Throughout the world she has many followers. Throughout the globe there are churches and icons with the image of *Saint Barbara.* They acknowledge her many good deeds.

She loves to have her name spoken by humanity. She accepts offerings. Her favorites are candles, cigars, apples (delicious), rum, and "gold" jewelry.

You will find many items of gold jewelry in stores and on the internet with her image on it. These will reflect power, strength and protection in your life.

Remember that the *House of Chango* is the head of the *Seven African Powers*. They are the right hand of GOD.

Chango is the saint of lightening and thunder. She is very powerful and will intervene on your behalf. She is the warrior princess known as *Saint Barbara*. When she was a thirteen year old virgin *Saint Barbara* converted to

Christianity. Her father beheaded her himself for her beliefs. Though she called out to GOD, he/she wanted the beautiful *Barbara* in heaven with him/her.

GOD promised *Barbara* that if any mortal called out the name of *Saint Barbara* when they were in "crisis" they would be saved.

Both *Saint Barbara* and *Chango* are ready to protect and guide YOU if you believe. They have given me permission to take you on my life's journey. I was told to share my fondest experiences with you. There is so much more I wish I could say to you. But I was told not to. Not yet. I will soon my friend.

Very Soon.

Not now. Not yet.

Soon, my friend – be patient.

Very soon I will be able to share details of the rituals that I've learned. I will tell you how to use flowers, candles, cigars, and incense and prayer cards. I will share my knowledge of how to attain enlightenment, unrequited love, do a self-cleaning, house-cleansing, and to protect you. Oh, and how to do so much more.

What I will do NOW, with permission of the *saints*, is to give YOU a gift. The pictures on the front and back of this book show YOU my altar. You now have MY blessings and may now have access to my power for a moment in time.

Once you finish reading this book, YOU and only YOU may place the book in a spot to be viewed.

Look up and speak with respect. For the next SEVEN days YOU and only YOU may speak to the *Saints* with my permission.

First, identify yourself. Use your birth name. Second, say that YOU have the permission of *Ronnie Gale Turbane, #1 of Saint Barbara* to <u>make a request</u>.

YOU have paid the price for a request by buying this book.

My gift to you is the ability to make **ONE REQUEST** of *Saint Barbara or Chango.*

You must make your request within 7 days after finishing a <u>complete reading</u> of this book.

You may make a request only for yourself. It may only be for good and not evil. You may NOT ask to hurt or harm anyone. You may ask for strength, protection or to defeat your enemies. You may NOT ask for great wealth. Though you may ask for money to help you survive.

Stand in front of either the front or back cover of this book. Speak to *Saint Barbara* or *Chango*, whichever one you need to.

<u>This is my gift to you</u>.

Use this gift wisely.

If it is your destiny, your request will come to pass within seven days. If you do not receive exactly what you have requested please remember *GOD's greatest gifts are "unanswered prayers"*.

<u>Have a blessed day</u>.